To

Eve

From

Terry

365 Smiles a Year For Friends

FaithP☆int™
PRESS

365 Smiles a Year For Friends

Scripture taken from the HOLY BIBLE: NEW INTERNATIONAL VERSION®. NIV®. Copyright © 1973, 1978, 1984 by International Bible Society. Used by permission of The Zondervan Corporation.

The "NIV" and "New International Version" trademarks are registered in the United States Patent and Trademark Office by International Bible Society.
All rights reserved.

ISBN: 1-58173-491-3

Book design by Pat Covert

Printed in China

365 *Smiles a Year For Friends*

FaithP✦int™
PRESS

A friend comes to mind with a smile and memories of a sweet fragrance, like a rose pressed in the pages of a favorite book.

Unknown

And in the sweetness of friendship let there be laughter and the sharing of pleasures. For in the dew of little things, the heart finds its morning and is refreshed.

Kahlil Gibran

There is no hope of joy except
in human relations.

Antoine de Saint-Exupéry

In loneliness, in sickness, in confusion-the mere knowledge of friendship makes it possible to endure, even if the friend is powerless to help. It is enough that they exist.

Pam Brown

No man is useless while he has a friend.

Robert Louis Stevenson

How rare and wonderful is that
flash of a moment when we realize
we have discovered a friend.

William E. Rothschild

You are beginning to see that any man to whom you can do favor is your friend, and that you can do a favor to almost anyone.

Mark Caine

Laughter is not a bad beginning for a friendship, and it is the best ending for one.

Henry Ward Beecher

He who wishes to secure the good of others has already secured his own.

Confucius

We cannot tell the precise moment when friendship is formed. As in filling a vessel drop by drop, there is at last a drop which makes it run over. So in a series of kindness there is, at last, one which makes the heart run over.

James Boswell

I awoke with devout thanksgiving
for my friends.

Ralph Waldo Emerson

I thank you, God, in heaven,
for friends.

Margaret Sangster

Those who bring sunshine
into the lives of others cannot keep
it from themselves.

Sir James M. Barrie

Love is like the wild-rose briar;
friendship is like the holly-tree.
The holly is dark when the rose
briar blooms,
But which will bloom most
constantly?

Emily Brontë

Our friends should be companions who inspire us, who help us rise to our best.

Joseph B. Wirthlin

Celebrate the happiness that friends are always giving. Make every day a holiday and celebrate just living!

Amanda Bradley

I cannot even imagine where I would be today were it not for that handful of friends who have given me a heart full of joy.

Charles R. Swindoll

It's the little things that matter, that add up in the end, with the priceless thrilling magic found only in a friend.

Elizabeth Dunphy

Friends are the ones who lift us from our feet when our wings forget how to fly.

Unknown

Winning has always meant much to me, but winning friends has meant the most.

Babe Didrikson Zaharias

Good friends are good for
your health.

Irwin Sarason

In a friend you find a second self.

Isabelle Norton

The friend within the man is that part of him which belongs to you and opens to you a door which never, perhaps, is opened to another. Such a friend is true, and all he says is true; and he loves you even if he hates you in other mansions of his heart.

Antoine de Saint-Exupéry

The best time to make friends is
before you need them.

Ethel Barrymore

January 25

Two friends, two bodies with
one soul inspired.

Homer

Fear makes strangers of people
who would be friends.
Shirley MacLaine

Yes, we are [friends], and I do like to pass the day with you in serious and inconsequential chatter. I wouldn't mind washing up beside you, dusting beside you, reading the back half of the paper while you read the front.

Jeanette Winterson

Friendship is love,
without his wings.

Lord Byron

January 29

A friend is a feeling of
forever in the heart.

Unknown

In the sweetness of friendship,
let there be laughter and
sharing of pleasures.
Kahlil Gibran

There is a scarcity of friendship,
but not of friends.
Thomas Fuller

February 1

True friendship is like sound health; the value of it is seldom known until it is lost.

Charles Caleb Colton

There is one friend in the life of each of us who seems not a separate person, however dear and beloved, but an expansion, an interpretation, of one's self, the very meaning of one's soul.

Edith Wharton

A man's growth is seen in the successive choirs of his friends.

Ralph Waldo Emerson

The best way to mend a broken heart is time and girlfriends.

Gwyneth Paltrow

February 5

When you choose your friends, don't be short-changed by choosing personality over character.

W. Somerset Maugham

You cannot shake hands
with a clenched fist.
Indira Gandhi

True friendship brings sunshine to
the shade and shade to the sunshine.

Thomas Burke

When we honestly ask ourselves which person in our lives means the most to us, we often find that it is those who, instead of giving advice, solutions, or cures, have chosen rather to share our pain and touch our wounds with a warm and tender hand.

Henri Nouwen

Friendship is like money-easier
made than kept.

Samuel Butler

Ah, how good it feels!
The hand of an old friend.

Henry Wadsworth Longfellow

Mighty proud I am that I am able to have a spare bed for my friends.

Samuel Pepys

February 12

Hold a true friend with both
your hands.

Nigerian Proverb

Make new friends, but keep the old;
one is silver, and the other's gold.

Unknown

There is nothing better than the encouragement of a good friend.

Katharine Butler Hathaway

Too often we underestimate the power of a touch, a smile, a kind word, a listening ear, an honest compliment, or the smallest act of caring, all of which have the potential to turn a life around.

Leo Buscaglia

When you judge another, you do not
define them. You define yourself.

Wayne Dyer

Woe to a man who falls down and has no one to pick him up.

Unknown

A friend is a person with whom I may be sincere. Before him I may think aloud. I am arrived at last in the presence of a man so real and equal, that I may drop even those undermost garments of dissimulation, courtesy, and second thought.

Ralph Waldo Emerson

Friendship needs no words;
it is solitude delivered from the
anguish of loneliness.

Dag Hammarskjold

A friend is known when needed.

Leo Buscaglia

The language of friendship is not words but meanings.

Henry David Thoreau

You cannot be friends upon any other terms than upon the terms of equality.

Woodrow Wilson

Where there are friends,
there is wealth.

Titus Muccius Plautus

Friendship consists in forgetting what one gives, and remembering what one receives.

Alexandre Dumas

In everyone's life, at some time, our inner fire goes out. It is then burst into flame by an encounter with another human being. We should all be thankful for those people who rekindle the inner spirit.

Albert Schweitzer

Old friends is always best, 'less you can catch a new one that's fit to make an old one out of.

Sarah Orne Jewett

Friends are treasures.

Horace Burns

No man can be happy without a friend, nor be sure of his friend till he is unhappy.

Thomas Fuller

Though friendship is not quick to burn, it is explosive stuff.

May Sarton

What we do for ourselves dies with us. What we do for others and the world remains and is immortal.

Albert Pine

The heart has its reasons, of which reason knows nothing.

Pascal

To ease another's heartache is to forget one's own.

Abraham Lincoln

The most beautiful discovery true friends make is that they can grow separately without growing apart.

Elisabeth Foley

It is easier to forgive an enemy
than to forgive a friend.

William Blake

One's friends are that part of
the human race with which one
can be human.

George Santayana

A friend knows the song in my heart and sings it to me when my memory fails.

Donna Roberts

You can always tell a real friend. When you've made a fool of yourself, he doesn't feel you've done a permanent job.

Laurence J. Peter

Friendship is unnecessary, like philosophy, like art. It has no survival value; rather it is one of those things that give value to survival.

C. S. Lewis

Constant use will not wear ragged
the fabric of friendship.

Dorothy Parker

The greatest good you can do for
another is not just share your riches,
but reveal to them their own.

Benjamin Disraeli

Do not protect yourself by a fence,
but rather by your friends.

Czech Proverb

He who has a thousand friends
has not a friend to spare, and he
who has one enemy will meet
him everywhere.
Ali ibn-Abi-Talib

One should count each
day a separate life.

Lucius Annaeus Seneca

You cannot do a kindness too soon,
for you never know how soon it will
be too late.

Ralph Waldo Emerson

A good friend is cheaper
than therapy.

Unknown

But if the while I think on thee,
dear friend

All losses are restored,
and sorrows end.

William Shakespeare

March 18

A true friend is one who
thinks you are a good egg even
if you are half-cracked.
Bernard Meltzer

It is the friends you can call up at 4 a.m. that matter.

Marlene Dietrich

A true friend never gets in your way unless you happen to be going down.

Arnold Glasgow

She is a friend of mind .... The pieces I am, she gather them and give them back to me in all the right order. It's good, you know, when you got a woman who is a friend of your mind.

Toni Morrison

Nothing but heaven itself is better than a friend who is really a friend.

Titus Muccius Plautus

March 23

A real friend is someone who would feel lost if you jumped on a train or in front of one.

Unknown

Silences make the real conversations between friends. Not the saying but the never needing to say is what counts.

Margaret Lee Runbeck

We are not enemies, but friends. We must not be enemies. Though passion may have strained, it must not break our bonds of affection. The mystic cords of memory will swell when again touched as surely they will be by the better angels of our nature.

Abraham Lincoln

It is not so much our friends'
help that helps us, as the
confidence of their help.

Epicurus

Before borrowing money from a friend, decide which you need most.

American Proverb

The tender friendships one gives up, on parting, leave their bite on the heart, but also a curious feeling of a treasure somewhere buried.

Antoine de Saint-Exupéry

A true friend reaches for your hand and touches your heart.

Unknown

Two are better than one,
because they have a good return for
their work: If one falls down, his
friend can help him up. But pity the
man who falls and has no one to
help him up!

Ecclesiastes 4:9-10

We are keenly aware of the faults of our friends, but if they like us enough, it doesn't matter.

Mignon McLaughlin

A true friend unbosoms freely, advises justly, assists readily, adventures boldly, takes all patiently, defends courageously, and continues a friend unchangeably.

William Penn

A good friend is a connection to life-a tie to the past, a road to the future, the key to sanity in a totally insane world.

Lois Wyse

I always felt that the great high privilege, relief, and comfort of friendship was that one had to explain nothing.

Katherine Mansfield

A friend is someone who is always there and will always, always care.

Unknown

A friend can tell you things you
don't want to tell yourself.

Frances Ward Weller

There is magic in long-distance friendships. They let you relate to other human beings in a way that goes beyond being physically together and is often more profound.

Diana Cortes

Of what shall a man be proud, if he is not proud of his friends?

Robert Louis Stevenson

A friend accepts us as we are yet helps us to be what we should.

Unknown

The friend who holds your
hand and says the wrong thing is
made of dearer stuff than the one
who stays away.

Barbara Kingsolver

I value the friend who for me finds time on his calendar, but I cherish the friend who for me does not consult his calendar.

Robert Brault

'Tis a great confidence in a friend to tell him your faults; greater to tell him his.

Benjamin Franklin

The best rule of friendship is
to keep your heart a little softer
than your head.

Unknown

If it's very painful for you to criticize your friends-you're safe in doing it. But if you take the slightest pleasure in it, that's the time to hold your tongue.

Alice Duer Miller

Many a person has held close, throughout their entire lives, two friends that always remained strange to one another, because one of them attracted by virtue of similarity, the other by difference.

Emil Ludwig

Without wearing any mask we
are conscious of, we have a special
face for each friend.

Oliver Wendell Holmes

I don't need a friend who changes when I change and who nods when I nod; my shadow does that much better.

Plutarch

A single rose can be my garden ... a single friend, my world.

Leo Buscaglia

If you would lift me up, you must be on higher ground.

Ralph Waldo Emerson

The best way to cheer yourself up is
to try to cheer somebody else up.

Mark Twain

Don't judge each day by the harvest you reap, but by the seeds you plant.

Robert Louis Stevenson

The friend is the man who knows all about you and still likes you.

Elbert Hubbard

I do not wish to treat friendships daintily, but with the roughest courage. When they are real, they are not glass threads or frost-work, but the solidest thing we know.

Ralph Waldo Emerson

A friend loves at all times.

Proverbs 17:17

A friend in need is a friend indeed.

Latin Proverb

A loyal friend laughs at your jokes
when they're not so good and
sympathizes with your problems
when they're not so bad.

Arnold Glasgow

A contented mind is the
greatest blessing a man can enjoy
in this world.

Joseph Addison

My best friend is the one who
brings out the best in me.

Henry Ford

Friends are those rare people who ask how you are and then wait for the answer.

Unknown

Friends are born, not made.

Henry Adams

Friends have all things in common.

Plato

Grief can take care of itself, but to get the full value of joy you must have somebody to divide it with.

Mark Twain

A good friend remembers what we were and sees what we can be.

Unknown

Fortune and love befriend the bold.
Ovid

Three keys to more abundant living: caring about others, daring for others, sharing with others.

William Arthur Ward

May 5

There is no joy in possession
without sharing.

Erasmo da Rotterdam

When we share – that is poetry in
the prose of life.

Sigmund Freud

A cloudy day is no match for a
sunny disposition.
William Arthur Ward

Cheerfulness and contentment are great beautifiers and are famous preservers of youthful looks.

Charles Dickens

Count your joys instead of your woes; count your friends instead of your foes.

Irish Proverb

You can tell more about a person by what he says about others than you can by what others say about him.

Leo Aikman

To measure the man,
measure his heart.

Malcolm Forbes

Treasure your relationships,
not your possessions.

Anthony J D'Angelo

If you wish your merit to be known,
acknowledge that of other people.

Asian Proverb

There are big ships and small ships.
But the best ship of all is friendship.

Unknown

The friend who can be silent with us in a moment of despair or confusion, who can stay with us in an hour of grief and bereavement, who can tolerate not knowing, not curing, not healing, and face with us the reality of our powerlessness-that is a friend who cares.

Henri Nouwen

The most important single
ingredient in the formula of
success is knowing how to get along
with people.

Theodore Roosevelt

Friends are kisses blown to
us by angels.

Unknown

A friend is one of the nicest things
you can have, and one of the best
things you can be.

Douglas Pagels

Friendship isn't a big thing. It's a million little things.

Unknown

Only your real friends will tell you
when your face is dirty.

Sicilian Proverb

The antidote for fifty enemies
is one friend.

Aristotle

May 22

Each friend represents a world in us, a world possibly not born until they arrive, and it is only by this meeting that a new world is born.

Anais Nin

May 23

A friend is someone who is there for you when he'd rather be anywhere else.

Len Wein

Truth and tears clear the way to a deep and lasting friendship.

Unknown

True friendship is never serene.

Marquise de Sevigne

I will speak ill of no man, and speak all the good I know of everybody.

Benjamin Franklin

Thus nature has no love for solitude and always leans, as it were, on some support; and the sweetest support is found in the most intimate friendship.

Marcus Tullius Cicero

It is a sweet thing, friendship,
a dear balm,
A happy and auspicious bird of calm.

Percy Bysshe Shelley

If all my friends were to jump off a bridge, I wouldn't jump with them. I'd be at the bottom to catch them.

Unknown

The happiest moments my heart knows are those in which it is pouring forth its affections to a few esteemed characters.

Thomas Jefferson

When friends stop being frank and useful to each other, the whole world loses some of its radiance.

Anatole Broyard

The making of friends, who are real friends, is the best token we have of a man's success in life.

Edward Everett Hale

Do not save your loving speeches
For your friends till they are dead;
Do not write them on their
tombstones,
Speak them rather now instead.

Anna Cummins

The best way to keep your friends is to not give them away.

Wilson Mizner

A good friend is hard to find, hard to lose, and impossible to forget.

Unknown

Promise you won't forget me,
because if I thought you would,
I'd never leave.

Winnie the Pooh

I'd like to be the sort of friend that you have been to me. I'd like to be the help that you've been always glad to be; I'd like to mean as much to you each minute of the day, as you have meant, old friend of mine, to me along the way.

Edgar A. Guest

Friends are the sunshine of life.

John Hay

Friendship improves happiness and abates misery by doubling our joy and dividing our grief.

Joseph Addison

June 9

Friendship is not diminished by distance or time, by imprisonment or war, by suffering or silence. It is in these things that it roots most deeply. It is from these things that it flowers.

Pam Brown

Life is so much friendlier with two.

Winnie the Pooh to Piglet

What do we live for, if it is
not to make life less difficult
for each other?

George Eliot

Time isn't what makes a friendship last. It's love and devotion that keeps the tie between souls.

Unknown

June 13

Friendship is the only cement that will ever hold the world together.

Woodrow Wilson

Never shall I forget the days I spent with you. Continue to be my friend, as you will always find me yours.

Ludwig van Beethoven

Walking with a friend in the
dark is better than walking
alone in the light.

Helen Keller

A cheerful friend is like a sunny day
spreading brightness all around.

John Lubcock

May the sun always shine on your windowpane; may a rainbow be certain to follow each rain. May the hand of a friend always be near you; may God fill your heart with gladness to cheer you.

Irish Blessing

A man of many companions may come to ruin, but there is a friend who sticks closer than a brother.

Proverbs 18:24

Friendship is the golden thread that
ties the heart of all the world.

John Evelyn

Friends aren't jumper cables. You don't throw them into the trunk and pull them out for emergencies.

Unknown

A true friend is the greatest of all blessings, and that which we take the least care to acquire.

Francois de la Rochefoucauld

A true friend is one who overlooks your failures and tolerates your success!

Doug Larson

People are like stained glass windows. They sparkle and shine when the sun is out, but when the darkness sets in, their true beauty is revealed only if there is a light from within.

Elizabeth Kubler-Ross

The road to a friend's house
is never long.

Danish Proverb

Friendship is the strangest but greatest thing in the world ....
My friends are my heart, my soul, my fun, my laughter, tears, love, and my life.

Kate Tierney

True friendship comes when silence
between two people is comfortable.

Dave Tyson Gentry

The greatest sweetener of human life is friendship. To raise this to the highest pitch of enjoyment is a secret which but few discover.

Joseph Addison

June 28

Friendship is the inexpressible comfort of feeling safe with a person, having neither to weigh thoughts nor measure words.

George Eliot

What is a friend? I will tell you.
It is someone with whom
you dare to be yourself.

Frank Crane

June 30

There is nothing on this earth more
to be prized than true friendship.
St. Thomas Aquinas

Your friends are very
precious things;
Their love is like the rarest gem.
But friends are hard to find and keep
Unless you are a friend to them.

Ann Cragg

Many people will walk in and out of your life, but only true friends will leave footprints in your heart.

Eleanor Roosevelt

A friend is someone who lets you have total freedom to be yourself.

Jim Morrison

When it hurts to look back, and you're scared to look ahead, you can look beside you and your best friend will be there.

Unknown

Friends are helpful not only because they will listen to us, but because they will laugh at us.

Will Durant

One of the best ways to keep friendship is to return it.

Unknown

He's my friend that speaks well of me behind my back.

Thomas Fuller

The holy passion of Friendship is of so sweet and steady and loyal and enduring a nature that it will last through a whole lifetime, if not asked to lend money.

Mark Twain

Friendship is a horizon that expands
whenever we approach it.

E. R. Hazlip

True happiness consists not in the multitude of friends, but in their worth and choice.

Samuel Johnson

The glory of friendship is not the outstretched hand, nor the kindly smile, nor the joy of companionship; it is the spiritual inspiration that comes to one when he discovers that someone else believes in him and is willing to trust him with friendship.

Ralph Waldo Emerson

I keep my friends as misers do their treasure, because, of all the things granted us by wisdom, none is greater or better than friendship.

Pietro Aretino

Peace and friendship with all mankind is our wisest policy, and I wish we may be permitted to pursue it.

Thomas Jefferson

Perhaps the most delightful friendships are those in which there is much agreement, much disputation, and yet more personal liking.

George Eliot

July 15

A blessed thing it is for any man or woman to have a friend, one human soul whom we can trust utterly, who knows the best and worst of us, and who loves us in spite of all our faults.

Charles Kingsley

'Tis the privilege of friendship to talk nonsense, and have her nonsense respected.

Charles Lamb

With true friends ... even water drunk together is sweet enough.

Chinese Proverb

A friend is someone who dances with you in the sunlight, and walks with you in the shadows.

Unknown

For how many things, which for our own sake we should never do, do we perform for the sake of our friends?

Marcus Tullius Cicero

A friend is one who takes
me for what I am.

Henry David Thoreau

A friend is what the heart
needs all the time.

Henry Van Dyke

We are all travellers in the wilderness of this world, and the best we can find in our travels is an honest friend.

Robert Louis Stevenson

We cannot always assure the future of our friends; we have a better chance of assuring our future if we remember who our friends are.

Henry Kissinger

There is no friend like an old friend who has shared our morning days, no greeting like his welcome, no homage like his praise.

Oliver Wendell Holmes

The difficulty is not so great to die
for a friend, as to find a friend
worth dying for.

Homer

At the shrine of friendship
never say die; let the wine of
friendship never run dry.
Victor Hugo

To hear complaints with patience, even when complaints are vain, is one of the duties of friendship.

Samuel Johnson

Friendship is one of the sweetest joys of life. Many might have failed beneath the bitterness of their trial had they not found a friend.

Charles Haddon Spurgeon

The proper office of a friend is to side with you when you are wrong. Nearly anybody will side with you when you are right.

Mark Twain

A friend shares the good
times and helps out by listening
during the bad times.

Molly Oliver

July 31

Don't pity the girl with one true friend. Envy her. Pity the girl with just a thousand acquaintances.

Katie Obenchain

Tart words make no friends; a spoonful of honey will catch more flies than a gallon of vinegar.

Benjamin Franklin

Friends are the most important part of your life. Treasure the tears, treasure the laughter, but most importantly, treasure the memories.

Dave Brenner

Like branches of a tree we grow in different directions, yet our roots remain as one. Each of our lives will always be a special part of the other's.

Unknown

Some friends come and go like a season. Others are arranged in our lives for good reason.

Sharita Gadison

A true friend is someone you can disagree with and still remain friends. For if not, they weren't true friends in the first place.

Sandy Ratliff

I believe in angels, the kind heaven sends. I am surrounded by angels, but I call them my best friends.

Unknown

The friendship isn't worth the tears
unless the friend is.

Kellina Filbin

Friends are like stars. You don't always see them, but you know they're always there.

Hulali Luta

Trouble is a sieve through which we sift our acquaintances. Those too big to pass through are our friends.

Arlene Francis

Nations will rise and fall. Wars will be lost and won. Lives will begin and end, but a true friend is eternal.

Jon Koroluk

It doesn't matter what people say.
To me, you're always a somebody.

Sam Baker

People love others not for who they are, but for how they make us feel.

Irwin Federman

When you look around and your world is crumbling, and when you think no one loves you, your best friend is the one to run to.

Meaghan West

Friends are always friends no matter how far you have to travel back in time. If you have memories together, there is always a piece of your friendship inside your heart.

Kellie O'Connor

True friends are always
together in spirit.

Lucy Maud Montgomery

If I could reach up and hold a star
for every time you made me smile,
the entire evening sky would be in
the palm of my hand.

Unknown

Friends are like windows through which you see out into the world and back into yourself .... If you don't have friends, you see much less than you otherwise might.

Merle Shain

If we would build on a sure foundation in friendship, we must love friends for their sake rather than for our own.

Charlotte Brontë

A friendship can weather most things and thrive in thin soil, but it needs a little mulch of letters and phone calls and small, silly presents every so often – just to save it from drying out completely.

Pam Brown

Little friends may prove
great friends.

Aesop

A friend is someone who
sees through you and still
enjoys the view.

Wilma Askinas

August 22

From quiet homes and
first beginning,
Out to the undiscovered ends,
There's nothing worth the wear
of winning,
But laughter and the love of friends.

Hilaire Belloc

You never really know someone
until you have been their friend.

Walker Best

For memory has painted this
perfect day
With colors that never fade,
And we find at the end of a
perfect day
The soul of a friend we've made.

Carrie Jacobs Bond

Life has no blessing like a
prudent friend.

Euripides

The rule of friendship means there should be mutual sympathy between them, each supplying what the other lacks and trying to benefit the other, always using friendly and sincere words.

Marcus Tullius Cicero

Yes, we must ever be friends; and of all who offer you friendship let me be ever the first, the truest, the nearest, and dearest!

Henry Wadsworth Longfellow

Friendship is neither a formality nor a mode: it is rather a life.

David Grayson

No birth certificate is issued when friendship is born. There is nothing tangible. There is just a feeling that your life is different and that your capacity to love and care has miraculously been enlarged without any effort on your part.

Steve Tesich

A friend is somebody you want to be around when you feel like being by yourself.

Barbara Burrow

Treat your friends as you do
your pictures, and place them in
their best light.

Jennie Jerome Churchill

Since there is nothing so well worth having as friends, never lose a chance to make them.

Francesco Guicciardini

Give me one friend, just one, who meets the needs of all my varying moods.

Esther M. Clark

It is better to have one friend of great value than many friends who are good for nothing.

Laertius Diogenes

Wherever we are, it is our friends
that make our world.
Henry Drummond

If instead of a gem, or even a flower, we should cast the gift of a loving thought into the heart of a friend, that would be giving as the angels give.

George E. MacDonald

We cherish our friends not for their ability to amuse us, but for ours to amuse them.

Evelyn Waugh

September 7

It is by chance we met; by choice we became friends.

Unknown

If I had to choose between betraying my country and betraying my friend, I hope I should have the guts to betray my country.

Edward Morgan Forster

Indeed, we do not really live unless we have friends surrounding us like a firm wall against the winds of the world.

Charles Hanson Towne

A friend is someone who, upon seeing another friend in immense pain, would rather be the one experiencing the pain, than to have to watch their friend suffer.

Amanda Grier

Depth of friendship does not depend on length of acquaintance.

Rabindranath Tagore

No distance of place or lapse of time
can lessen the friendship of those
who are throughout persuaded of
each other's worth.

Robert Southey

September 13

One of the most beautiful qualities
of true friendship is to understand
and to be understood.

Lucius Annaeus Seneca

September 14

What brings joy to the heart is not so much the friend's gift as the friend's love.

St. Alfred of Rievaulx

A friend drops their plans when you're in trouble, shares joy in your accomplishments, feels sad when you're in pain.

Doris Wild Helmering

A friend is someone who makes me
feel totally acceptable.

Ene Riisna

One does not make friends.
One recognizes them.

Garth Henrichs

September 18

Be slow in choosing a friend, but slower in changing him.

Scottish Proverb

Blessed are they who have the gift of making friends, for it is one of God's best gifts. It involves many things, but above all, the power of going out of one's self, and appreciating whatever is noble and loving in another.

Thomas Hughes

To attract good fortune, spend a new coin on an old friend, share an old pleasure with a new friend, and lift up the heart of a true friend by writing his name on the wings of a dragon.

Chinese Proverb

The greatest gift of life is friendship,
and I have received it.

Hubert H. Humphrey

God gives us our relatives. Thank
God we can choose our friends.

Michel Eyquem de Montaigne

Those truly linked don't need correspondence. When they meet again after many years apart, their friendship is as true as ever.

Deng Ming-Dao

I am treating you as my friend,
asking you to share my present
minuses in the hope that I can ask
you to share my future pluses.

Katherine Mansfield

September 25

No friendship can cross the path of our destiny without leaving some mark on it forever.

Francois Mauriac

Remember, the greatest gift is not found in a store nor under a tree, but in the hearts of true friends.

Cindy Lew

Go through your phone book, call people, and ask them to drive you to the airport. The ones who will drive you are your true friends. The rest aren't bad people; they're just acquaintances.

Jay Leno

The rain may be falling hard outside,
But your smile makes it all alright.
I'm so glad that you're my friend.
I know our friendship will never end.

Robert Alan

September 29

One who looks for a friend without faults will have none.

Unknown

Who finds a faithful friend,
finds a treasure.

Jewish Proverb

Friendship is essentially a
partnership.
Aristotle

A companion loves some agreeable qualities which a man may possess, but a friend loves the man himself.

James Boswell

Friendship is a strong and habitual inclination in two persons to promote the good and happiness of one another.

Eustace Budgell

A sympathetic friend can be quite
as dear as a brother.

Homer

It is not what you give your friend,
but what you are willing to give
him that determines the quality
of friendship.

Mary Dixon Thayer

True friendship is a plant of slow growth, and must undergo and withstand the shocks of adversity, before it is entitled to the appellation.

George Washington

Are we not like two volumes of
one book?

Marceline Desbordes-Valmore

Let us be grateful to people who make us happy. They are the charming gardeners who make our souls blossom.

Marcel Proust

If you're alone, I'll be your shadow. If you want to cry, I'll be your shoulder. If you want a hug, I'll be your pillow. If you need to be happy, I'll be your smile. But anytime you need a friend, I'll just be me.

Unknown

The bond that links your true family is not one of blood, but of respect and joy in each other's life. Rarely do members of one family grow up under the same roof.

Richard Bach

October 11

The influence of each human being on others in this life is a kind of immortality.

John Quincy Adams

I would rather have a million friends than a million dollars.

Edward Vernon Rickenbacker

Of all the music that reached farthest into heaven, it is the beating of a loving heart.

Henry Ward Beecher

One discovers a friend by chance, and cannot but feel regret that 20 or 30 years of life may have been spent without the least knowledge of him.

Charles Dudley Warner

What sunshine is to flowers, smiles are to humanity. These are but trifles, to be sure; but scattered along life's pathway, the good they do is inconceivable.

Joseph Addison

What we have once enjoyed we can never lose. What we love deeply becomes a part of us.

Helen Keller

Strangers are just friends
waiting to happen.

Napoleon

October 18

You're a happy fellow, for you'll give happiness and joy to many other people. There is nothing better or greater than that.

Ludwig van Beethoven

Friendship is the source of the greatest pleasures, and without friends, even the most agreeable pursuits become tedious.

St. Thomas Aquinas

Friendship was given by nature to be an assistant to virtue, not a companion to vice.

Marcus Tullius Cicero

Since you get more joy out of giving joy to others, you should put a good deal of thought into the happiness that you are able to give.

Eleanor Roosevelt

October 22

Sometimes your joy is the source of your smile, but sometimes your smile can be the source of your joy.

Thich Nhat Hanh

Trust men and they will be true to you; treat them greatly, and they will show themselves great.

Ralph Waldo Emerson

We must indeed all hang together, or most assuredly we shall all hang separately.

Benjamin Franklin

October 25

We would rather be in the company of somebody we like than in the company of the most superior being of our acquaintance.

Frank Swinnerton

We've grown to be one soul-two parts; our lives so intertwined that when some passion stirs your heart, I feel the quake in mine.

Gloria Gaither

One who knows how to show and to accept kindness will be a friend better than any possession.

Sophocles

Our chief want in life is somebody
who shall make us do what we can.

Ralph Waldo Emerson

Friends keep the young out of mischief; to the old they are a comfort and aid in their weakness, and those in the prime of life, they incite to noble deeds.

Aristotle

October 30

Friends are as companions on a journey, who ought to aid each other to persevere in the road to a happier life.

Pythagoras

The ultimate measure of a person is not where they stand in moments of comfort and convenience, but where they stand in times of challenge and controversy.

Martin Luther King Jr.

The way to love anything is to realize that it might be lost.

G. K. Chesterton

Every woman should have one
friend who always makes her laugh
and one who lets her cry.

Unknown

A good friend can tell you what is the matter with you in a minute. He may not seem such a good friend after telling.

Arthur Brisbane

A friend is someone who will help you move. A real friend is someone who will help you move a body.

Unknown

Consult your friend on all things, especially on those which respect yourself. His counsel may then be useful where your own self-love might impair your judgment.

Lucius Annaeus Seneca

In prosperity our friends know us; in adversity we know our friends.

John Churton Collins

We are advertis'd by our
loving friends.

William Shakespeare

A despairing man should have the devotion of his friends, even though he forsakes the fear of the Almighty.

Job 6:14

A true friend knows your weaknesses but shows you your strengths; feels your fears but fortifies your faith; sees your anxieties but frees your spirit; recognizes your disabilities but emphasizes your possibilities.

William Arthur Ward

I've learned that all a person has in life is family and friends. If you lose those, you have nothing, so friends are to be treasured more than anything else in the world.

Trey Parker

Living is having ups and downs and
sharing them with friends.
Matt Stone

We secure our friends not by
accepting favors but by doing them.

Thucydides

November 13

And say my glory was I
had such friends.

William Butler Yeats

Don't ask of your friends what you yourself can do.

Quintus Ennius

The essence of true friendship is
to make allowances for
another's little lapses.
David Storey

Listening is a magnetic and strange thing, a creative force. The friends who listen to us are the ones we move toward. When we are listened to, it creates us, makes us unfold and expand.

Karl Menninger

You don't just luck into things as much as you'd like to think you do. You build step by step, whether it's friendships or opportunities.

Barbara Bush

A friend should be one in whose understanding and virtue we can equally confide, and whose opinion we can value at once for its justness and its sincerity.

Robert Hall

Friendship is a living thing that lasts only as long as it is nourished with kindness, empathy, and understanding.

Unknown

November 20

Perfume and incense bring joy to
the heart, and the pleasantness of
one's friend springs from his
earnest counsel.

Proverbs 27:9

Friends need not agree in everything or go always together, or have no comparable other friendships of the same intimacy. On the contrary, in friendship union is more about ideal things.

George Santayana

False friendship, like the ivy, decays and ruins the walls it embraces, but true friendship gives new life and animation to the object it supports.

Richard Burton

I get by with a little help
from my friends.

John Lennon

Of all the things which wisdom provides to make life entirely happy, much the greatest is the possession of friendship.

Epicurus

Friends are God's way of
taking care of us.

Unknown

To know someone here or there with whom you can feel there is understanding in spite of distances or thoughts expressed, that can make life a garden.

Johann Wolfgang von Goethe

There comes that mysterious meeting in life when someone acknowledges who we are and what we can be, igniting the circuits of our highest potential.

Rusty Berkus

Every gift from a friend is a wish for your happiness.

Richard Bach

Old friends pass away; new friends appear. It is just like the days. An old day passes; a new day arrives. The important thing is to make it meaningful: a meaningful friend-or a meaningful day.

Dalai Lama

A friend who is far away is sometimes much nearer than one who is at hand. Is not the mountain far more awe-inspiring and more clearly visible to one passing through the valley than to those who inhabit the mountain?

Kahlil Gibran

Let us learn to show our friendship for a man when he is alive and not after he is dead.

F. Scott Fitzgerald

Friends make life a lot more fun.
Charles R. Swindoll

The beauty of friendship is
in security.

Robert Frost

The comfort of having a friend may be taken away-but not that of having had one.

Lucius Annaeus Seneca

A friend is one that knows you as you are, understands where you have been, accepts what you have become, and still, gently allows you to grow.

William Shakespeare

But friendship is the breathing rose,
with sweets in every fold.
Oliver Wendell Holmes

December 7

I find friendship to be like wine, raw when new, ripened with age, the true old man's milk and restorative cordial.

Thomas Jefferson

Friendship is almost always the union of a part of one mind with the part of another; people are friends in spots.

George Santayana

A friend is a hand that is always holding yours, no matter how close or far apart you may be.

Unknown

The ideal friendship is to feel as one while remaining two.

Anne Sophie Swetchine

A friend encourages your dreams and offers advice–but when you don't follow it, they still respect and love you.

Doris Wild Helmering

Friends are those rare people
who ask how we are and then wait
to hear the answer.
Ed Cunningham

In poverty and other misfortunes of life, true friends are a sure refuge.

Aristotle

Can miles truly separate us from friends? If we want to be with someone we love, aren't we already there?

Richard Bach

Without friends the world is but
a wilderness.

Sir Francis Bacon

The best time to make friends is before you need them.

Ethel Barrymore

How delightful to find a friend in everyone.

Joseph Brodsky

Two persons cannot long be friends if they cannot forgive each other's little failings.

Jean de la Bruyere

The rule of friendship means there should be mutual sympathy between them, each supplying what the other lacks and trying to benefit the other, always using friendly and sincere words.

Buddha

Friends are all that matter.

Frank Burgess

December 21

The world is round so that friendship may encircle it.

Pierre Teilhard de Chardin

What sweetness is left in life, if you take away friendship? Robbing life of friendship is like robbing the world of the sun. A true friend is more to be esteemed than kinsfolk.

Marcus Tullius Cicero

What is a friend? I will tell you
it is someone with whom you
dare to be yourself.

Frank Crane

A man's friendships are one of the best measures of his worth.

Charles Darwin

December 25

Greater love has no one than this, that he lay down his life for his friends.

John 15:13

True friendship is when two friends can walk in opposite directions, yet remain side by side.

Unknown

Friendship without self interest is one of the rare and beautiful things in life.

James Francis Byrnes

We will be friends until forever,
just you wait and see.

Winnie the Pooh

Hold on to the friends you care about, and since we don't have a remote control to mute someone or just change the channel, pick your friends carefully.

Unknown

I used to think that friends were the people that you could laugh and talk to. Now I know that friends aren't that. They're the people that touch your heart.

Kate Tierney

Whoever is happy will make others happy, too.

Mark Twain